BUILDING A
DEMOCRATIC
NATION

GOVERNMENTS IN TRANSITION

By Gretchen E. Matthews

CLOSE UP PUBLISHING

CLOSE★UP®
F O U N D A T I O N

Close Up Publishing

Director
George W. Dieter

Managing Editor
Amy E. Tarasovic

Senior Editor
Charles R. Sass

Writer
Gretchen E. Matthews

Manager of Art, Production, and Scheduling
Tisha L. Finniff

Graphic Designer
Deborah A. Stalford

Supervisor of Editorial Support and Scheduling
Lucy Keshishian

Copyeditor and Proofreader
Margaret White

Photo Researcher
Matt Payne

Close Up Foundation
Stephen A. Janger
President and Chief Executive Officer

The Close Up Foundation, a nonprofit, nonpartisan, civic education organization, informs, inspires, and empowers people to exercise the rights and accept the responsibilities of citizens in a democracy. Close Up connects individuals of all ages to their communities and institutions through challenging educational programs and products. By building partnerships with the education community, the private and philanthropic sectors, and all branches and levels of government, Close Up makes civic participation a dynamic and meaningful experience.

Close Up Publishing, a branch of the Close Up Foundation, develops books, teachers' guides, video documentaries, and other materials that encourage critical thinking skills and stimulate interest in current issues, government, international relations, history, and economics. To find out more about Close Up's original and timely resources, call 800-765-3131 or visit www.closeup.org/pubs.htm.

Close Up Foundation
44 Canal Center Plaza
Alexandria, VA 22314-1592
www.closeup.org

Cover Photo: AP Photo/David Guttenfelder

CONTENTS

PART I

WHAT IS DEMOCRACY?

Democracy can be defined as a concept of government which rests on the idea that a society's citizens have the right to govern themselves. Democracy is government by the people, whose will is exercised either directly or through elected representatives. Based upon the principles of self-determination and political equality, a democracy is a state in which all sovereign power (ultimate authority) resides with the people. Citizens participate in the government, enjoy voting rights, and control the government's agenda. In modern usage, a democracy is also a state in which all citizens have equal rights and enjoy civil liberties—regardless of their social rank or privilege—and where free and fair elections are held regularly. Beyond these general ideas, however, democracy is a complex topic.

For centuries, political theorists have debated the origins and future of democracy. Most have agreed that democracy is an ever-changing form of government, varying from nation to nation, generation to generation.

ANCIENT DEMOCRACIES

Long before modern democracy developed, a few popular governments—governments of self-rule by the people, or the *populus*—existed in various forms in small communities around the known world. Families, villages, and towns that believed in political equality for certain members of society, usually free men, embraced some democratic ideals.

Athens. Most scholars trace the origins of large-scale democracy to Greece in the first half of the fifth century B.C. At that time, Greece was a conglomeration of city-states, each having its own government. The Greeks coined the term

The legislatures of some modern-day democracies greatly resemble the early Roman Senate.

demokratia, or democracy, from the Greek words *demos* (the people) and *kratos* (meaning strength, power, or rule) to describe their governing system. In Athens, the largest of the Greek city-states, the government was a direct democracy. Free men owning property, a small percentage of the total population, held the office of citizen and were members of a single sovereign assembly, the *Ecclesia*, which met about ten times per year to formulate and vote on city policy. Participation in the *Ecclesia* was a serious matter and was considered a citizen's duty. Athens's democracy lasted more than a century, but in 400 B.C., the city was conquered by the militaristic and authoritarian city-state of Sparta. After these events, democracy disappeared from ancient Greece.

Rome. Around the same time that the Athenian democracy existed, another popular government arose in the city-state of Rome. The Romans called their system a republic, from the Latin words *res* (a thing or assembly) and *publicus* (public). Like the Athenians, the Romans held a legislative assembly to discuss and determine policy, but unlike Athens, the Roman republic was a representative democracy. In a representative democracy, the people elect individuals to serve at a legislative assembly on their behalf. For about two hundred years, Rome's government was unicameral—composed of one chamber called the Senate. The Senate, also known as the Forum for its meeting place, was attended by representatives elected from the upper class—the aristocracy. By the third century B.C., however, the plebeians—lower-class citizens who were small farmers, merchants, tradesmen, and skilled workers—had become a significant economic force. The plebeians fought for their right to participate in the government as well, and in time, they achieved political equality and were able to elect their own representatives. The Roman legislature then became bicameral—composed of two chambers: the Senate (representatives of the aristocracy), and the Assembly (representatives of the plebeians). In time, the forces of war, military domination, corruption, and civil unrest weakened the Republic, leaving it vulnerable to takeover by strong autocratic emperors.

The Roman republic fell to autocratic rule around 44 B.C.

THE EMERGENCE OF MODERN DEMOCRACY

While the basic ideas of democracy, such as citizen participation and consent of the governed, existed in the popular rule of Athens and Rome, neither city-state's government was truly "by the people." A large proportion of each city's population, namely women and members of the lower classes, as well as slaves and free noncitizens, were excluded. Today's democracies are more inclusive—ideally, all citizens of a democratic nation have the right to participate in the governing process. Modern democracies are also designed to preserve citizens' individual rights. Yet, it took the world more than 2,000 years to learn to practice democracy this way. Most scholars agree that the principles of modern democracy—such as popular sovereignty and the recognition of individual rights—were born in England and developed with the growth of the English Parliament.

England. In 1215, English feudal lords forced King John to sign the Magna Carta (Latin for "Great Charter"). The Magna Carta marked the beginning of England's journey to popular government, and was significant for a number of reasons. It was the first written statement to declare the rule of law by limiting the power of a monarch and making the monarch subject to the law in the same way as other citizens. The Magna Carta also proclaimed the rights of the governed. Initially designed only to protect the lords' feudal privileges, the document did little or nothing for the common people. Yet it was written in broad terms. Therefore, the principles it laid out—such as the right to fair treatment before the law, judgment by one's peers, and the right to hold private property—were eventually accepted as the rights of all individuals. After the Magna Carta was signed, English law gradually changed to protect the rights of the governed.

Later in the thirteenth century, democracy in England took a great leap forward when King Edward I established a loosely organized representative legislature. Edward I frequently called and consulted with assemblies of individuals from all walks of life: barons, bishops, abbots, earls, knights, and even burgesses (townspeople). Over time, these assemblies grew to become the English Parliament, a bicameral legislature composed of the House of Lords and the House of Commons. The upper house, the House of Lords, was comprised of representatives from the aristocracy who inherited their seats through their families, while the lower house, the House of Commons, was made up of representatives elected by the common people.

The sharing of power between the king and Parliament evolved over centuries, largely because of the increasing economic power of the middle and working classes. As these classes prospered, their representatives in Parliament grew more powerful. English kings gave a great deal of their power to Parliament in exchange for the ability to tax the prosperous lower classes who had been increasing their wealth over hundreds of years.

By the seventeenth century, the English Parliament had become significantly more influential. The Parliament won the king's agreement to several legislative reforms and contracts by giving him an annual income from the tax revenues the Parliament collected. Among the most important contracts the king signed was the Petition of Right of 1628. It confirmed that monarchs, like all English citizens, were subject to English law; it declared the right of the people not to be taxed without representation in the English Parliament; and it declared that no person could be imprisoned arbitrarily (without lawful reason). Although King Charles I signed this document, he was not willing to comply with it; he went so far as to dissolve Parliament from time to time when it disagreed with him.

The tension between Parliament and Charles I led to seven years of civil war beginning in 1642. In the end, Parliament's forces and their leader, Oliver Cromwell, defeated the king's army and attempted to create a republic. However, Cromwell also grew displeased with the distribution of power between himself and Parliament. He dissolved the legislative assembly and appointed himself "Lord Protector," but he died a few years later. In 1660, the reinstated Parliament invited Charles II, the son of Charles I, to ascend the throne.

In 1685, Charles II died and his Roman Catholic brother, James II, became king. From 1685 to 1688, James II alienated his overwhelmingly Protestant nation by promoting Catholicism. Disgruntled Protestants, in a 1688 uprising known as the "Glorious Revolution," forced James to give up the crown. Parliament then offered the throne to William of Orange, the Protestant son-in-law of James II. As a condition of his rule, however, William was forced to sign the Declaration of Rights, a parliamentary document later enacted as the Bill of Rights.

The English Bill of Rights codified citizens' rights as they had evolved over the past five centuries and specified certain other rights as well, including freedom to assemble without restriction or permission; freedom to address grievances to the king and Parliament (petition); freedom of speech for members of Parliament; and the right not to be excessively fined, punished, or wrongfully imprisoned. The U.S. Bill of Rights, created 100 years later, was modeled, in large part, after this document.

Natural Rights. While economic issues, such as taxation, motivated the rise of representative government in Great Britain, other factors also influenced the process. The Enlightenment—a period of great intellectual debate and growth during the seventeenth and eighteenth centuries—led to an increased study of individuals' rights. Philosophical ideas of the Enlightenment influenced political thinkers, shaping their ideas about the nature of law, government, and citizens' rights. Enlightenment ideas inspired America's war for independence, influenced the formation of the U.S. government, and formed the foundation of today's Western democratic systems. Three important philosophers of the time were John Locke, Baron de Montesquieu, and Jean Jacques Rousseau.

Locke. In 1690, the English philosopher John Locke published *Two Treatises on Government,* in which he advocated a social contract to protect the rights of the governed, enable freedom of thought for all individuals, and promote the right of citizens to own property. Locke also used this book to advance his most influential ideas regarding natural rights. Natural rights are rights that humans recognize through the powers of reason. They are endowed by nature, inherent in a person's being, and universal to all humans. Life and liberty, for example, are considered natural rights. Locke believed it was the responsibility of government to protect such rights. The power of legislators, he wrote, "is limited to the public good of the society. It is a power that hath no other end but preservation, and therefore can never have a right to destroy, enslave, or designedly impoverish the subjects. . . ." Locke believed that the test of a good government is its ability to ensure that the people's natural rights are not sacrificed by the government's action or inaction when appropriate.

Montesquieu. Another philosopher who greatly influenced the development of individual rights was Baron de Montesquieu, a Frenchman, who built upon Locke's theories in his 1748 book, *De l'esprit des lois* (The Spirit of the Laws). He declared that a government, to fully protect the rights of citizens and avoid arbitrary rule (random rule, independent of the law), must be divided into branches separated according to function. Montesquieu described a system of three branches that are all subject to the rule of law, as each branch is composed of citizens who are all treated equally under the law. A government subject to the rule of law is a limited government.

Rousseau. Finally, Jean Jacques Rousseau, also a French philosopher, elaborated on Locke's theories of natural rights in his book, the *Social Contract* (1762). Rousseau's work explored the ways in which a government must be restricted by law from infringing upon individuals' rights and freedoms.

DEMOCRACY IN AMERICA

We hold these Truths to be self-evident, that all men are created equal, that they are endowed by their Creator with certain unalienable Rights, that among these are Life, Liberty and the pursuit of Happiness. That to secure these rights, Governments are instituted among Men, deriving their just powers from the consent of the governed, That whenever any Form of Government becomes destructive of these ends it is the Right of the People to alter or to abolish it, and to institute new Government, laying its foundation on such principles and organizing its powers in such form, as to them shall seem most likely to effect their Safety and Happiness.

—U.S. Declaration of Independence

The long course of development of representative democracy in England, combined with the thoughts of the Enlightenment philosophers, influenced colonial leaders in forming the American republic. In 1776, the founders signed their names to the Declaration of Independence, risking their lives and fortunes in the name of freedom to establish a new nation independent of Great Britain and its king. The declaration's opening words, "When in the Course of human events . . . ," and its proclamations of equality, self-government, and the right to abolish tyrannical government were directly inspired by the thinkers of the Enlightenment, and they mark the culmination of hundreds of years of debate regarding the role of government in protecting people's natural rights. The colonists presented the declaration to King George III as a list of grievances against him, offering natural rights as justification for rebellion.

At the time the Declaration of Independence was signed, however, and throughout the American Revolution, the colonists did not have a plan for governing the United States. Thus, while the Declaration of Independence listed the colonists' natural rights, it did not specify the form the new national government would take.

The Articles of Confederation. In the interim between the drafting of the Declaration of Independence and the signing of the Constitution, the thirteen states were loosely unified under a document called the Articles of Confederation. The Confederation was designed as a "firm league of friendship" between the states, each of which had declared itself an independent sovereign entity. However, the Articles of Confederation proved ineffective as a form of national government. The written agreement did not provide the authority to collect taxes, maintain a military, control foreign or interstate commerce, enforce its own laws, or resolve disputes between states.

Because of these shortcomings, representatives from the thirteen states met in 1787 to form a new and more effective national government—one that would embrace the democratic principle of popular sovereignty, yet would also be limited in power, protecting both citizens' and states' rights. The plan they agreed to became the U.S. Constitution.

The Constitution. The preservation of states' rights was extremely important to many of the Constitution's framers. In order to protect the states' sovereignty, a new plan for sharing power, called federalism, was born. Federalism is the idea that states, while members of the nation at large, have the right to retain certain powers independent of the national government. In practice, federalism also creates unity between the states by limiting the national government's power. Since its inception in the U.S. Constitution, federalism has been employed by other democratic governments throughout the world.

The Constitution's framers were also concerned with planning a national government. They were unsure how to design a government that would best protect the rights of the governed. With many options before them, the framers turned back to the Enlightenment philosophers for guidance.

Calling upon Montesquieu's idea of a separation of powers, the framers created a system of government with three branches. The legislative assembly, or Congress, was conceived as a bicameral system. In the Senate, all states were to be represented equally. In the House of Representatives, representation would be divided according to the population of each state. The bicameral system satisfied the small states' demands for equal power in the Senate, while giving the larger states a chance to wield influence through their greater representation in the House. Senators were to be chosen by the state legislatures, while Representatives were to be chosen through popular elections in each state.

The U.S. Constitution was written in Philadelphia, Pennsylvania, in the summer of 1787. Thirty-nine of the forty-two delegates present signed the Constitution before the Convention adjourned.

The president, as head of the executive branch, would be chosen based on the results of a national election and serve independent of the legislative branch. The president would have the power to administer the policies of the national government.

The judicial branch, with the Supreme Court at the top of lower federal courts, was given the final authority to interpret national law. To strengthen the judicial branch, the Constitution stated that judges—appointed by the president and approved by the Senate—be given lifetime appointments and salaries that could not be reduced. These two mechanisms were to guarantee the judges' independence by protecting them from the influence of the other branches. A few years later in the landmark case of *Marbury v. Madison* (1803), the Supreme Court declared that the Constitution also grants the judicial branch the power of judicial review—

the ability to declare an act of Congress or the president unconstitutional.

To ensure that no branch became too powerful, the Constitution set forth a system of checks and balances between the legislative, executive, and judicial branches. Checks and balances enabled the branches to veto or overrule one another's actions in specific ways, thereby preventing unjust rule from endangering citizens' rights.

The Bill of Rights. Although the Constitution protected some individual rights, many of the framers and the states they represented wanted to add a list of rights. They argued that in a pure democracy, a simple majority could outlaw unpopular speech, religion, and other rights that many Americans considered God-given and indispensable to citizens' freedom. Pure democracy allows the majority to rule entirely, without

"As a man is said to have a right to his property, he may be equally said to have a property in his rights."

—James Madison, 1792

These words are inscribed in the Madison Memorial Hall, Library of Congress James Madison Memorial Building.

ments guarantee individuals certain liberties and prohibit the federal government from infringing upon them. The Fifth through Eighth Amendments define and protect the rights of individuals accused of crimes or otherwise involved in legal disputes. The Ninth Amendment guarantees that any individual rights not stated in the Constitution cannot be taken away by the federal government. And finally, the Tenth Amendment reserves to the states and the people any powers not listed in the Constitution as powers of the federal government.

HOW DEMOCRACIES ARE ALIKE

Many forms of Government have been tried, and will be tried in this world of sin and woe. No one pretends that democracy is perfect or all-wise. Indeed, it has been said that democracy is the worst form of Government except all those other forms that have been tried from time to time.

—Winston Churchill

respecting individuals' rights and privileges. A bill of rights guaranteeing the freedoms of speech and religion, and the right to due process before the law (the protection of an individual's rights, especially when accused of a crime), would therefore protect individuals and the minority from the tyranny of the majority. These ideas stemmed directly from both Locke's and Rousseau's beliefs about the supremacy of individual rights over those of a government.

The Bill of Rights, the first ten amendments to the Constitution, was adopted in 1791. The first four amend-

As the framers of the U.S. Constitution learned, forming a representative democracy is difficult. Yet successful modern democracies have a number of things in common; most important, they value and recognize the importance of the following democratic ideas.

Popular Sovereignty. The core principle of any democracy is popular sovereignty, whereby the citizenry as a whole is the sovereign, or ultimate, authority of the nation. The nation's citizens together hold power over all elected government officials. If the people, the nation's citizens, are not considered the ultimate source of the government's power, the nation is not a democracy.

Free and Fair Elections. In a representative democracy, the will of the people is expressed through free and fair elections. Elections are free and open to all citizens of voting age, and citizens are politically equal—each individual's vote counts the same. Elections cannot be rigged or votes weighted to favor a candidate. Elected representatives are accountable to their constituents and may be voted out of office. In a democratic system, the people abide by the votes cast. If a nation's citizens do not abide by the votes cast, or if the elections are not free and fair, the will of the people will not be accurately represented by the outcome of the election.

In new democracies, citizens often need to be educated about the electoral process. Having only been ruled by others, many people in fledgling democratic nations do not realize the significance of their role as voters in the democratic process. Often, they fear punishment for expressing their ideas by casting ballots. Thus, one of the challenges a new democracy faces is to create a sustainable electoral process, so the nation's citizens ultimately bring the leaders they desire into power.

Rule of Law. The term rule of law is the principle of equal treatment before the law. It means that all citizens, whether or not they hold public office, are subject to the same laws in the same way. For a democratic nation to function, remain stable, and fully protect the rights of all its citizens, the rule of law must be acknowledged by the people and the government. Citizens of democracies must know and respect the law and understand that they will face consequences if they commit unlawful acts. Similarly, a democracy's legal system must also respect the rule of law, applying laws fairly and uniformly to all individuals.

When the rule of law is not established or respected, citizens' rights may be endangered by unchecked governmental power. The nation may also experience instability. In states where the rule of law is not acknowledged or understood, men and women can be arrested without reason, and individuals or groups may harm others without penalty.

Autonomy. A fully democratic nation is independent of all outside powers. In other words, for a democratic nation to have true sovereignty, it must not be subject to any over-arching government or regime, such as a former colonial power.

Inclusive Citizenship. Citizenship is the status accorded to members of a state or nation, especially one with a democratic form of government, which guarantees an individual full civil rights and certain privileges. Generally, democratic nations grant citizenship and its benefits to all persons born in that nation or those persons who are of a certain age and are willingly, permanently, and legally living within the nation's boundaries.

Countries trying to install democracy often deal with complex citizenship issues. For example, eastern European nations making the transition to democracy have in many cases denied citizenship to the Roma (also called Gypsies), a nomadic European ethnic group. Some eastern

In the United States, citizens often take for granted how easy it is to vote. Once people turn 18, they simply register as voters and cast their ballots at their local polling station on election day. But in new democracies, citizens often do not know how to vote, and officials do not know how to run elections. Today, nongovernmental organizations (NGOs) serve throughout the world as civic educators, teaching people to register as voters, evaluate candidates and their positions, and conduct fair elections.

One such NGO is the International Foundation for Election Systems (IFES). Since 1987, IFES has worked in more than 100 countries to help develop fair electoral systems. In nations such as Georgia, Paraguay, Moldova, Nigeria, and the Philippines, IFES has instructed people in every aspect of the electoral process. IFES workers have taught political party volunteers to make posters to advertise their candidates, assisted with the development of ballot forms, and trained election officials to tally votes and publish election results promptly. IFES has even helped election staff check voting equipment, to make sure it works and is safe from tampering.

IFES has been particularly effective in showing ordinary citizens how to participate in the election process. In Indonesia, IFES produced an instructional video to teach voters about their responsibilities during elections. The video was broadcast on national television prior to the 1999 elections, and more than three-quarters of Indonesian voters watched. In 2000, IFES hosted democracy camps for high school students in Ukraine and Kyrgyzstan, and it created new civics textbooks for schools in Kazakhstan.

European nations cite Gypsies' lack of long-term residency within their nations as reason to deny them citizenship and its corresponding rights, responsibilities, and privileges.

Universal Suffrage. Modern democracies offer suffrage—the right to vote—to all citizens of a certain age. Universal suffrage is a fairly recent development in the history of democracy. For example, in the United States, only white, male property owners were allowed to vote until after 1800. Women received the right to vote through the Nineteenth Amendment, not ratified until 1920. And although the Fifteenth Amendment to the Constitution gave black Americans the right to vote, certain states created barriers to suffrage such as poll taxes and literacy tests. It was not until 1965 that Congress passed the Voting Rights Act, which finally outlawed discrimination at the voting booth.

Freedom of Expression, Information, and Association. People living in a modern democracy have also come to expect certain freedoms associated with natural rights. Such freedoms include the freedom of expression, through speech, press sources, or other media outlets, as well as the freedom of information and association. These freedoms enable citizens to speak, move, educate, and organize themselves without interference from the government. Some democratic nations, however, place restrictions upon the freedoms of expression, information, and association, such as only protecting some forms of speech, or not releasing certain information to the public.

HOW DEMOCRACIES DIFFER

While all modern democracies embrace such democratic notions as popular sovereignty and free and fair elections, democracies may have different government structures.

Constitutions. The guiding principles of a democratic nation are commonly written down in one founding document, a constitution. A constitution sets forth the supreme law of the land—the system of fundamental laws and principles upon which the nation or state relies. A constitution provides stability, anchoring the methods of decisionmaking, accountability, and representation that a democratic government will use to serve its citizens.

While a constitution sets forth a nation's supreme law, it can usually be modified as changing circumstances warrant. Altering a constitution, however, is generally difficult. The principles upon which a constitution are based are meant to endure. In the United States, the Constitution cannot be amended without widespread support from the people speaking through Congress and their state legislatures. More than 5,000 amendments to the U.S. Constitution have been proposed, yet only 27 have been added, the first 10 of which were adopted in 1791.

Not all democracies have constitutions. The democratic governments of Great Britain, Israel, and New Zealand,

for example, have never had formal written constitutions. In these nations, the constitution is the whole body of law, which includes laws determined by the legislature and by customs, as well as laws determined by court cases. As the body of law is changed by customs, judicial rulings, and the nation's legislature, the constitution of the nation is changed.

Regardless of whether or not a democracy accepts a formal, written constitution, if it abides by the democratic principles of popular sovereignty and limited government, the democracy is considered a constitutional government.

The Assembly. The form of the legislature varies among representative democracies.

In most democracies, freedom of expression is protected by law. Here, nurses in Warsaw, Poland, protest low pay and job cuts in front of the parliament building.

AP Photo/Czarek Sokolowski

Bicameral legislatures are common, but some nations, such as Israel, have chosen a unicameral, or one-house, legislature instead. Still others have modified their governments over time. Since the 1950's, Norway, Sweden, Finland, Denmark, Iceland, and New Zealand have abolished their upper houses, and Great Britain's upper house—the House of Lords—has little power today.

Democratic governments also differ at the legislative level in the ways they determine representation. In some national assemblies, the number of representatives from any region is determined by that region's population. In other cases, each district or region receives the same number of representatives. Still others decide representation based on political party membership.

The Administration. Representative democracies usually choose their chief executives through one of two systems: a parliamentary system or a presidential system. In a parliamentary system, the chief executive is elected by the legislature and can be removed by it. Great Britain, Canada, and Japan are examples of parliamentary systems. The chief executive in a presidential system is popularly elected for that office, is not responsible to the legislative branch, and can be removed from office only by the legislature under extraordinary circumstances. The United States, France, and Palau are examples of nations with presidential systems.

Heads of State. Most modern democracies, including the United States, are republics, with elected heads of state, such

as presidents or prime ministers. Other representative democracies have a king or queen as head of state. These types of democracies are called constitutional monarchies. Today, most monarchs serve in a ceremonial function only. Examples of modern constitutional monarchies are Great Britain, the Netherlands, and Thailand.

The Courts. The responsibility of a democratic nation's courts is to uphold and interpret the national laws. Democracies select justices for their courts in various ways, usually by appointment with approval from an executive or legislature. Tenure for federal judges also varies between democracies. In the United States, justices appointed to the Supreme Court serve for life. Other democratic nations such as Germany, Italy, and Japan appoint judges to lengthy, yet limited terms.

Many modern democratic systems also use the process of judicial review, whereby the judicial branch may declare an act of the legislative or administrative branch unconstitutional. The extent of judicial review varies between democratic nations. In the United States, the U.S. Supreme Court has the power to declare any action of the president or Congress unconstitutional. In some democracies, however, the highest court may have judicial review only over state legislation.

Referendums. Some modern representative democracies have retained a form of direct democracy by holding national referendums—votes by all citizens, not just elected representatives—on national

In a democracy, the assembly writes the nation's laws. Pictured here is Germany's Reichstag parliament in Berlin.

AP Photo/POOL

elections or writing a constitution does not make a nation a democracy because these actions alone will not sustain a democratic government. Democratic governments rely on the help of informed and involved citizens to govern effectively. Therefore, citizens must be involved in the transition process, focusing their attention on three critical areas: (1) building democratic state institutions, (2) creating a civil society, and (3) administering a fair electoral process. When advances in these areas are made simultaneously, democracy becomes an attainable goal.

issues. In Switzerland, for example, referendums are held frequently and are required for constitutional amendments. The U.S. Constitution makes no provision for national referendums, yet they are frequently held at the state and local levels. Many referendums are initiated by petition drives whereby the signatures of eligible voters can force an issue onto the ballot. In California, for example, enough signatures were gathered to force a vote in the November 2000 election on whether to require drug treatment programs and probation for certain convictions of drug possession.

BUILDING A DEMOCRATIC NATION

Nations making the transition to democracy understand the components of democracy and the options they have in creating their new governments. Yet building a democratic nation is not a simple, straightforward task. Holding

State Institutions. In new democracies, state institutions such as the courts, the military, the police, and local governments must be created in accordance with the rule of law to guarantee that they will protect the rights of the governed. All citizens, regardless of rank or privilege, must first recognize and respect the absolute rule of the law— meaning that each person is subject to the law in the same way all the time. Then, they must expect and demand the same respect for the absolute rule of the law from their leaders in state institutions. A constitution is generally drafted to set the laws, list the responsibilities of the state institutions, and outline the rights of the people.

In a democracy, elected officials must abide by the law and be accountable to the people. The courts must apply the law fairly and uniformly. Officers in the military and the police must understand and accept the scope of their responsibilities as protectors and defenders of citizens' rights. If the officials in state institutions do not conduct themselves in accordance with the law, the system will become corrupt and therefore unable to protect the rights of the nation's people at large.

Civil Society. Nations becoming democracies must also create a civil society to advocate for individuals' rights and look out for their best interests. Civil society refers to nongovernmental, not-for-profit independent associations that make use of the freedoms of expression and association to advance the well-being of citizens. For example, labor unions are part of civil society; they push for fair wages and governmental policies to protect workers. Civil society also includes apolitical groups such as churches and community centers, which aim to enhance citizens' daily lives.

A thriving civil society is an advantage to a nation trying to make the transition to democracy. It encourages citizens to be a part of the democratic process by showing them that, with effort, communities can come together to make positive changes in people's lives. When a nation's people organize themselves through civil society to approach state institutions with their concerns, democracy is strengthened.

Elections. Finally, new democracies must establish a free and open electoral process—the key to representative democracy. Running free and fair elections is a challenge for new democracies. Transitional governments, wary of losing power, may try to restrict access to the electoral process for both candidates and voters. Or, citizens may choose not to vote. People may decide not to vote for any number of reasons: they might not believe voting will make a difference; they might be unhappy with the choices in candidates; they might fear for their lives or safety;

Elections are essential to the formation of a democratic government. In December 1998, Nigeria held local elections, beginning the transition of Africa's most populous nation from military rule to democracy.

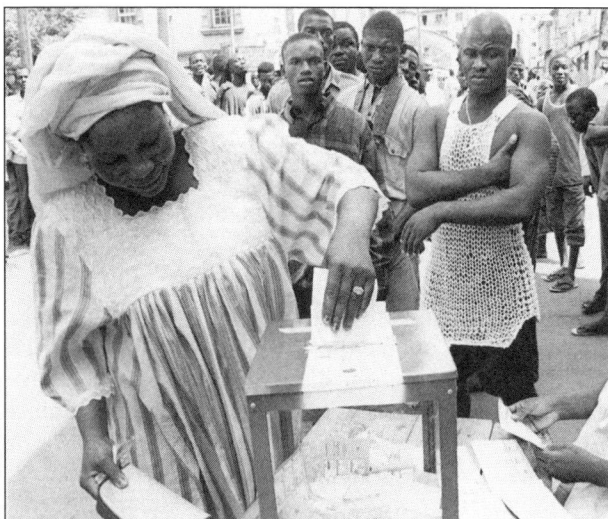

AP Photo/Peter Obe

or they might be unschooled, illiterate, and unaware of the choices before them. Nations in transition must search for ways to overcome the obstacles associated with apathetic or resistant voters. It is not easy. Even established, successful democracies like the United States struggle to get their citizens to go to the polls on election day.

AIDING NEW DEMOCRACIES

There are many challenges to preparing the foundation for democratic government. Thus, many efforts are made by established democracies to assist new democracies in their transition. From the early 1950s, U.S. foreign policy has included among its goals, aid to help countries establish democratic governments. In the 1960s, the Kennedy administration established the first formal U.S. democratic aid organizations, the United States Agency for International Development (USAID) and the Peace Corps. In the 1980s, Congress expanded U.S. democracy aid by establishing the National Endowment for Democracy (NED). In the 1990s, U.S. democratic aid was promoted most effectively through nongovernmental organizations (NGOs). Today, thousands of governmental and nongovernmental organizations, from many established democracies, give help in different forms to new democracies.

Aid organizations train legislators to handle specific political and economic issues. These organizations teach legislators the value of public hearings, the use of legislative committees, how to budget, and how to reach out to their

U.S. AID FOR OPPOSITION GROUPS

In an effort to promote democracy around the world, the United States often gives money and other forms of aid to opposition groups—parties trying to establish more democratic systems of government in their countries. Such assistance is meant to help these groups establish themselves and confront the injustices of repressive regimes. Aid to opposition groups is intended to level the playing field between democratic groups and antidemocratic groups, thus increasing the chances that democracy will take hold.

U.S. aid for opposition groups, however, is still a matter of debate. Some Americans believe it violates other nations' political sovereignty by tampering with the democratic process. They maintain that Americans would not want China, for example, to financially support political parties in the United States; therefore, U.S. agencies should not support parties in other nations. Others further contend that while U.S. agencies try to remain impartial, their assistance to certain groups demonstrates a desire to influence election outcomes. However, supporters of opposition-group assistance believe it is necessary to lay the groundwork for democracy and promote U.S. interests throughout the world.

constituents. Aid groups also train lawyers, judges, and police officers to uphold the nation's laws and apply them fairly. Military organizations also benefit from aid by learning how best to defend their nation and protect its citizens. In addition, aid groups often provide basic supplies and funding to state institutions for new libraries, office equipment, and information and communication systems.

The media in a democracy have the important job of informing citizens about the activities of their government. Thus, aid organizations teach journalists in transitioning nations how to report on legislative affairs and governmental policies. Some aid groups assist workers in forming unions to fight for workers' rights or support religious groups seeking to assemble for worship.

Aid organizations help citizens in new democracies understand the democratic process by teaching civics—the rights and responsibilities of citizenship. Civic education helps citizens comprehend how a democratic government works and shows them how to promote change in their nation's government when it does not meet their needs.

Finally, aid organizations work to strengthen a nation's infrastructure—the basic facilities upon which a nation relies to sustain itself and grow. Schools, roads, power plants, and transportation and communication systems are examples of infrastructure. A strong infrastructure provides people with more opportunities to increase their standard of living, a valued opportunity since many nations in transition suffer from economic decay or ruin.

The focus of aid programs has changed over the last few decades, as aid workers determine which methods work best to help communities and nations put democratic principles into action. Forming democratic nations takes time and often involves difficult choices. New democratic institutions, which are designed to be accountable to the people, often do not work smoothly when they are first created. Officials from the old state institutions may be a part of the new democratic institutions, and their old ways may undermine the progress toward democracy. Aid organizations help new democracies face these challenges, but they do not work alone. Emerging

Nongovernmental organizations (NGOs) work to help developing nations transition to democratic governments. Outside Phnom Penh, Cambodia, the Church World Service, one such NGO, constructed a school.

Kevin R. Morris/Corbis

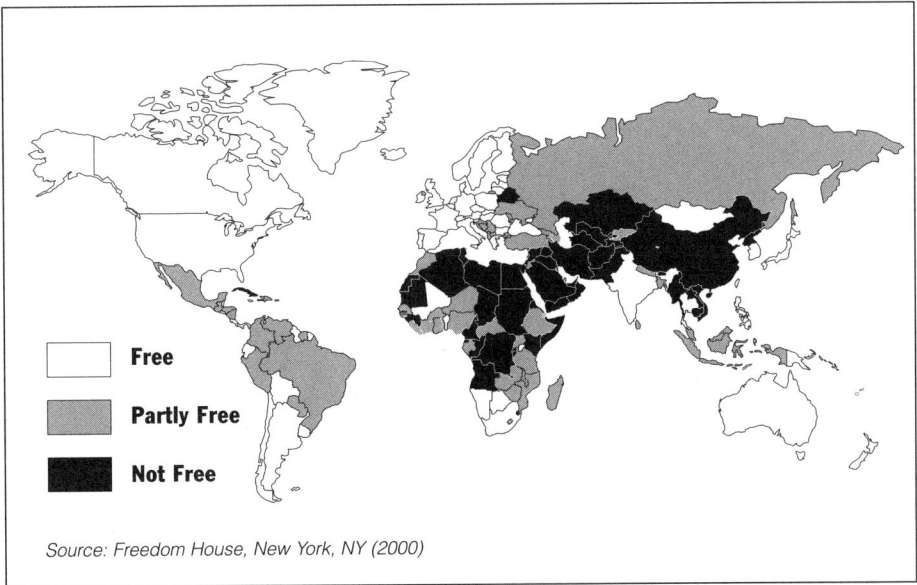

Free

Partly Free

Not Free

Source: Freedom House, New York, NY (2000)

Citizens in those countries marked "free" enjoy many political and civil freedoms. Citizens in "partly free" countries live with some restrictions on political rights and civil liberties, often due to corruption, weak rule of law, civil war, or ethnic strife. Citizens in "not free" countries are denied basic freedoms, and the political process is tightly controlled. Freedom House, an NGO which advocates for human rights and democratic practices around the world, produces this map annually.

democracies also receive assistance through international diplomacy.

Diplomacy. Most of the business between nations is conducted by representatives of nations—diplomats—who meet at conferences or have other less formal discussions to find solutions to global problems. Diplomacy has greatly helped democracy. Leaders from emerging democracies often use diplomatic relations to connect with more established democracies that in turn provide guidance and funding to assist the new democracies in their transitions. Similarly, an established democracy may work with a new democracy in the hope that, as the new democracy becomes more settled, trade or industry between the two countries may increase.

Exchanging democratic ideas through diplomacy leads to stable, profitable democracies around the world.

PART II

DEMOCRACY 2000

By the beginning of the twenty-first century, about 60 percent of the world's nations had adopted some form of democratic government. Even more remarkable is the fact that, from 1950 to 2000, the number of democracies around the world jumped from 22 to 120. Millions of people all over the world have embraced the democratic principles of freedom and justice, and democracy is taking root faster than many experts predicted.

SETTING THE STAGE

What brought about the recent global trend toward democracy? How can only twenty-two democracies grow to over five times as many in fifty years? The explanations are not the same for every new democracy, but most political scientists point to the gradual decline of totalitarian rule common in the early twentieth century; the fall of communism; the end of colonialism; an increase in world trade brought on by the trend toward capitalism; and improvements in education, communication, and transportation. Democracy has also been promoted by a growing interdependence among nations.

Totalitarianism in the Twentieth Century. The world of 1900 was much different from that of 2000. Many of the kings and queens who reigned at the beginning of the twentieth century lost their thrones and power as a result of World War I and related revolutions. But they were soon replaced by ruthless dictators and military rulers. Men like Adolf Hitler, Benito Mussolini, and Joseph Stalin came to power in Germany, Italy, and Russia by capitalizing on their nations' fears, nationalistic sentiments, and weak economic conditions. War lords ruled in Asia, and many military leaders in Latin America governed their nations with iron fists. Totalitarianism dominated much of the twentieth century. Totalitarianism is a form of government, usually headed by a dictator, that controls virtually every aspect of a country. Individual freedom under a totalitarian regime is almost nonexistent; the people are forced to live according to the will of the government.

As these totalitarian dictators sought to expand their spheres of influence and to carve out empires, they competed for power throughout the world. But they were not the first to practice imperialism—seizing control or sovereignty over another country. In fact, European democracies such as Great Britain, France, and the Netherlands had been holding colonies throughout Africa and Asia for many years. While the imperial nations were democratic, their colonies were not. Thus totalitarian dictators and colonial empires stifled democracy for much of the twentieth century.

The Decline of Colonialism. The fall of dictators in Germany, Italy, and Japan at the end of World War II opened the door for the development of real democracy in those countries and many of the regions they had dominated or intimidated with totalitarian rule. At this time, world colonialism was also ending. During the 1950s and 1960s, nations in Africa, Asia, and Latin America won their freedom from the European colonial powers. Many newly independent lands attempted to establish democracies; most failed. Within a few years of obtaining independence, many nations succumbed to native military rulers who

held power through the use of force. It was not until the last part of the twentieth century that many nations in Africa, Latin America, and Asia rejected their autocratic and corrupt governments and turned toward democracy.

The Cold War. While some dictators fell in 1945, another brand of totalitarianism, communism, quickly spread under the leadership of the Soviet Union. At the end of World War II, Europe was divided into the communist East and the democratic West by a heavily guarded border that British prime minister Winston Churchill dubbed, the "Iron Curtain." This division marked the beginning of the Cold War—a competition for power between the United States and the Soviet Union. For nearly forty years, the two superpowers fought the Cold War with propaganda, arms buildups, and the use of military and economic aid to win allies. Just as colonialism and military rulers stifled democracy in much of the world, so did the rivalry for influence between the U.S.-led West and the Soviet-led East.

The End of the Cold War. By the 1980s, decades of oppressive rule and faltering economies had created discontent in nations under Soviet control. In 1989, several communist eastern European nations began to revolt. The Soviets allowed them to hold elections, and the push for democracy began. In two short years, forty years of communist rule by the Soviet Union broke down. By 1991, the Soviet Union had disintegrated. The end of the Cold War signaled a new era of global relations. Over the course of the following decade, the nations previously under Soviet control or influence started to establish democratic governments and capitalist economies. Democracy was also beginning to take root in some anticommunist, but undemocratic, countries such as Guatemala, El Salvador, and South Korea, which had been receiving U.S. aid during the Cold War to prevent them from turning communist.

Capitalism and Democracy. A growing global interest in capitalism has helped spur the spread of democracy around the world. The economic system most common under a democratic political system, capitalism, is also called the free enterprise system. The most distinctive feature of capitalism is that private individuals and companies, rather than governments, own most of the property and decide what to do with it. Individuals are free to become entrepreneurs—to start and run their own businesses. These enterprises compete with one another for money. Capitalism is common under democratic systems because democratic governments guarantee private ownership, property rights, and the freedom for individuals to make their own decisions. Because capitalism promotes entrepreneurialism, capitalism also leads to the growth of the middle class, a group that has historically sustained democratic governments. In other words, democracy and capitalism generally go hand in hand. Communist or other totalitarian systems typically have rejected capitalism in favor of state control.

Socialism. Most communist countries practiced some form of socialism. Socialism is an economic philosophy based on the idea that wealth generated by economic activity should be equally dis-

FINDING PEACE?

What should a new democracy do with its old dictators? Should abusive former leaders be punished for atrocities committed under their regimes? Should victims be compensated for their suffering? If so, how? Newly democratic nations have found many different ways to answer these questions, some more extreme than others. For example, when communism fell in Romania in 1989, the Romanian people tried and executed their communist dictator, Nicolae Ceausescu, and his wife. When South Korea began its transition in 1987, strongman Chun Doo Hwan and his chosen successor, Roh Tae Woo, were thrown into prison. Years later, these two men were pardoned and released by the democratically elected president, Kim Dae Jung.

Still other nations have tried a third option. In 1994, South Africa established the Truth and Reconciliation Commission, whose objective was to promote national unity and reconciliation by publishing a full account of human rights violations committed under *apartheid*—the state-enforced segregation of black people and white people. By disclosing the causes and nature of abuses, as well as the names of those responsible, the commission hoped to restore victims' dignity and enable them to move forward with their lives. South Africa's commission has been credited with assisting the nation's democratic growth and has been replicated in other nations, such as Guatemala and Haiti.

tributed throughout society. A purely socialist economy rejects the capitalistic concepts of private ownership, free enterprise, and competition to make a profit.

Many noncommunist dictatorships also embraced socialism and rejected capitalism because the dictators could not stay in power if they allowed their people to think freely and openly or to engage in free enterprise. These regimes—as well as the old colonial powers—often banned free enterprise because they wanted to keep most of their country's or colony's wealth for themselves.

A major problem facing the leaders of today's emerging democracies is developing a plan to establish a successful capitalistic system. While they are excited about capitalism's prospects, they lack previous experience and adequate money to get their financial systems off the ground. Despite this disadvantage, new democracies are looking to embrace free enterprise with the same enthusiasm with which they have embraced free elections, free expression, and the rule of law.

Technology and Democracy. Technological innovation has also affected the development of new democracies. Even in early America, James Madison, Alexander Hamilton, and John Jay used technology by taking advantage of the printing press to spread their ideas about American democracy through *The Federalist Papers.* This series of essays was most influential in helping the states' citizens understand the significance and powers of the U.S. Constitution and the necessity of its ratification.

In the twentieth century, technology advanced dramatically. Radio and television brought live campaign coverage into peoples' homes, and telephones and typewriters made it easier for men and women to share their opinions with their representatives. Today, citizens use the Internet to assemble interest groups, create petitions for issues they care about, and inform themselves about legislative affairs. In the future, individuals may be able to vote on-line or hold on-line meetings to advocate for issues with other citizens living thousands of miles away. The technology of the

The Internet enables civil society organizations to promote democratic ideals around the world. Here, a Russian student browses the Internet in a Moscow cyber café.

AP Photo/Mikhail Metzel

twentieth century made information more accessible and gave the world's citizens the tools and inspiration they needed to rise up against oppressive regimes and demand government for and by the people.

ACROSS THE GLOBE: THE GROWTH OF DEMOCRACY IN FOUR NATIONS

A clear discussion of the spread of democracy in the world today requires casting a wide net that covers the ways in which building a new democracy varies from continent to continent and nation to nation. In this book, four nations have been chosen to illustrate the transition to democracy. Located in different regions of the world, each nation has had experiences similar to the countries around it. At the same time, these nations each face unique challenges and illustrate that the implementation of democracy is never the same in two places. Russia is overcoming communist rule and is struggling with an elite group of legislators and newly wealthy business owners who held power in the old Soviet Union and are now reluctant to give it up. In Venezuela, as in other South American democracies, the nation's citizens are in danger of losing the freedoms of democracy to an elected president aiming to strengthen his own power in an authoritarian manner. Uganda is trying to implement democracy in a way that will minimize the internal ethnic conflicts so common in Africa. Thailand illustrates how citizens marching in the streets can initiate democratic change in a part of the world unaccustomed to democracy. Together, these nations show how the transition to democracy can be both problematic and filled with opportunity.

RUSSIA

Climbing its way out from under 1,000 years of authoritarian rule and the ruin of a collapsed economy, Russia, the giant of Eurasia, is struggling to install democracy. While it has implemented a constitutional government that protects the individual rights of Russian citizens, the nation still faces the challenges that once threatened other postcommunist democracies in eastern Europe: a weak economy, impoverished citizens, government corruption, and the lack of a free press.

Boris Yeltsin, postcommunist Russia's first freely elected president, worked throughout the 1990s to reform the Russian government and establish a capitalist economy. Yeltsin recognized the benefits of constitutional government. In 1993, he oversaw the ratification of the Russian constitution, which provides for a bicameral legislature and a strong president with the power to appoint, with parliamentary approval, and dismiss a prime minister. (Russia is one of the few countries to have both a prime minister and a president. The president has more power.) The lower chamber of the legislature is called the Duma, and the upper chamber is called the Federation Council. Legislative elections in 1995 and 1999 and presidential elections in 1996 and 2000 brought the nation closer to establishing a government that reflects the will of the people; international observers deemed these elections free and fair.

Problems to Overcome. Although Russia has a constitution and holds regular, free, and fair elections, political power remains concentrated among Russia's oligarchs who used their positions as wealthy members of the old Soviet elite to gain insider information and unlawfully acquire much of Russia's state property when communism ended. The oligarchs and the government are widely suspected of corruption—allowing bribes to influence legislation and siphoning off government funds for personal use. The power of the oligarchs has hampered Russia's progress. Russia also has trouble with ruthless and powerful organized criminals operating outside the law.

International investors, intimidated by Russia's oligarchs and organized crime, withdrew much of their investment capital from Russia during the 1990s. As a result, the nation's economy stumbled and finally collapsed in 1998.

Russia's financial troubles have been made worse by the government's inability to collect taxes. The tax system is so haphazard, complicated, and unfair that citizens feel justified in refusing to pay. Also, citizens do not fear penalties for disregarding tax laws because the tax system is not enforced. Further, the federal government in Moscow lacks tax collection authority; Russia's regional governments control most tax collection. This means that the central government cannot raise funds to keep itself afloat or handle issues of national concern, such as feeding and clothing its vastly underfunded military. Faced with increasing international debt, a budget deficit, and rampant corruption among the oligarchs

and other political favorites, Russia's federal government is in desperate need of tax money to keep itself running. In recent years, it has even lacked the funds to pay its employees on time. Many have called for a new, simplified national tax system supported by enforcement procedures to bring the Russian government out of debt and promote the nation's economic growth and stability.

A New President. On December 31, 1999, Boris Yeltsin resigned the Russian presidency, replacing himself with his hand-picked prime minister, Vladimir Putin. Putin is a former member of the KGB, the old Soviet Union's national security and intelligence agency. He was officially elected president in March 2000 and has outlined plans for economic reform and consolidation of power at the national level. Putin's economic guidelines include commitments to protect private property rights, streamline state bureaucracy, cut unfair taxes and tariffs, and end welfare assistance for all but the poorest Russians. Experts suggest that these strategic economic reforms may rejuvenate the Russian economy, providing the framework for a stronger democracy. Entrepreneurialism would lead to increased wealth for the middle class, who would then consolidate their political strength and check the oligarchs' power.

While Putin's economic reforms appear favorable to some, democracy-development observers in Russia remain concerned about the president's efforts to strengthen his power and the power of the national government. The regional governors sitting in the Federation Council accepted Putin's proposal to eliminate their own seats by 2002. They also agreed to overhaul the federal tax code, giving up their control over billions of rubles in tax receipts every year. Under the new tax system, only the central tax service will have the power to collect and administer taxes. While some say the Federation Council's approval of the proposal will finally enable the government in Moscow to collect taxes and move itself out of debt, others fear Putin intends to restrict the regions' local sovereignty.

Repressed Civil Liberties. Civil liberties are another area of concern in Russia's emerging democratic system. Most of

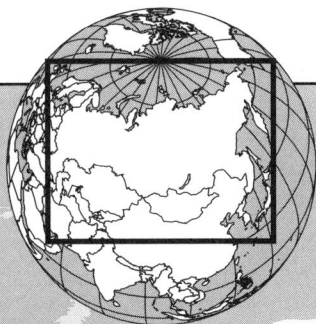

RUSSIA

HEAD OF STATE
President Vladimir Putin

HEAD OF GOVERNMENT
Acting Premier Mikhail Kasyanov

AREA
6,592,735 sq mi (slightly less than 1.8 times the size of the United States)

POPULATION
146,001,176

LIFE EXPECTANCY
male: 61.95 years/female: 72.69 years

INFANT MORTALITY RATE
20.33 deaths/1,000 live births

ANNUAL PER CAPITA INCOME
$4,200

LITERACY RATE
98%

GDP (GROSS DOMESTIC PRODUCT)
$620.3 billion

GDP GROWTH RATE
3.2%

INFLATION RATE (CONSUMER PRICES)
86%

INDUSTRIES
Mining (coal, oil, gas), ship and machine building, road and rail transportation equipment, communications equipment, and agricultural machinery

Source: *The World Factbook 2000,* published by the Central Intelligence Agency

Russia's media outlets are owned or funded by oligarchs who are closely allied with the Russian government. The Russian constitution provides for freedom of speech and the press, yet government officials pressure the media to ignore corruption and promote officials' interests.

Putin's administration has also cracked down on independent media groups. In May 2000, Russian authorities raided Media-MOST, the leading independent news organization, one that has occasionally been critical of the government. Many independent journalists in Russia fear such raids; they are also concerned for their personal safety and purposefully censor their work to protect themselves. A few journalists who criticized the war in Chechnya, a breakaway republic fighting for its independence, have disappeared. The government has also restricted journalists' access to the Chechen war zone to stifle media criticism.

Individual civil liberties are still restricted, largely because Russia's judiciary faces political interference, is underfunded, and is susceptible to corruption. Many criminal suspects do not receive fair trials or equal treatment before the law. Human Rights Watch—a U.S.-based NGO—has reported that torture is widely used as a means of extracting testimony from criminal suspects and that such testimonies are admissible in court.

Facing Russia's Future. Beyond these concerns, life in Russia is difficult for the average citizen. Since the fall of communism, death rates have risen because of alcoholism, rampant disease, and poor nutrition. The price of goods continues to rise rapidly. One in ten Russians is unemployed because the new capitalist economy has not yet created enough jobs. Of those who do work, many are underemployed, meaning that they have been forced to take low-paying jobs for which they are overly skilled.

Prospects for improving Russia's civil society to combat the ills of the corrupt government are dim. Most Russian citizens have not taken the initiative to organize themselves for democratic gain. Many are apathetic; they feel powerless to challenge the oligarchs and elected officials, or they believe that life in communist Russia was better. The Communist Party, with about 500,000 members countrywide, is still the nation's largest and most cohesive political force. Without jobs and income, citizens are concerned less about democratic change than about economic reform.

Nevertheless, many established democratic nations and lending organizations continue to give aid to Russia, particularly to assist with the growth of civil society. Policymakers in the United States disagree over whether to continue sending aid money to Russia. Some believe these funds are being misdirected to the military, or being misspent on other projects, and therefore are not meeting the social or economic needs of the people. Others say giving aid to Russia is crucial to stimulate economic growth. All agree, however, that a democratic Russia is necessary for global harmony.

President Putin promises to bring economic stability to Russia. Yet while his reforms might bring about positive changes, his actions might also further endanger citizens' rights. Much of the passion and enthusiasm that immediately followed the end of communism has faded, as citizens confront the painful realities of governmental transition throughout their country. With a history of totalitarian rule, human rights violations, a corrupt government, and a debilitated economy, Russia faces many problems on its way to establishing itself as a democratic nation.

VENEZUELA

Democratic progress in Latin America is often a process of one step forward, two steps back. Beginning in the 1960s, popular support for democracy in Latin America led to the creation of representative governments across the region. Over the next thirty years, however, most were replaced by authoritarian regimes, commonly military dictatorships. The region fell into economic, social, and political turmoil. The 1990s witnessed a return to elected civilian governments, as well as an emergence from the troubles that had plagued the region for decades: internal conflicts, high inflation, and economic decline. Many nations were also rebuilding their infrastructures—education, law enforcement, and transportation systems. Today, most Latin American nations want to complete their transitions to democracy, yet many challenges remain.

As the countries south of the United States turned to democracy, they also embraced capitalism, but with meager results. In most places, many in the middle and lower classes are too poorly educated to benefit from the new free enterprise economies. Throughout the region, the income gap between rich and poor, the widest of any region in the world, continues to grow. Violent crime, often closely linked to poverty, has also swept the region since the end of the Cold War. In light of these persistent problems, many Latin American citizens have begun to support undemocratic solutions. Analysts believe the greatest threat to democracy in Latin America right now is a slow turn toward autocratic government. The people of Peru and Venezuela, for example, have voted away the power of their representative governments because many believe those governments only serve the interests of the elite and privileged. Instead, many favor a return to military rulers who promise to help the less-privileged classes. Even elected leaders are ruling like dictators, supported by frustrated citizens looking for economic relief and opportunity. These citizens are angry about the corruption and ineptitude that characterize the current democratic systems and are terrified by rampant crime.

The Old Venezuela. The Republic of Venezuela was established in 1830, nine years after achieving independence from Spain under the leadership of Simon Bolivar, a national hero. With a history of colonial rule, military dictatorships, and prolonged periods of instability, Venezuela's past is similar to that of many other Latin American nations. Yet unlike some of its neighbors, it has enjoyed uninterrupted civilian rule since the early 1960s. Venezuela's constitution, created in 1961, provided for a president and a bicameral congress, both elected to five-year terms.

Until 1993, politics in Venezuela were dominated by two parties. But in 1993, the congress removed the corrupt Venezuelan president, Carlos Andres Pérez. That same year, a new president—Rafael Caldera—was elected by the National Convergence Party, a coalition of parties from both the left and the right. However, under Caldera's administration, many civil liberties were suspended, violent crime and social unrest mounted, and some national banks collapsed. In 1998, Hugo Chávez—who had led two coups in 1992 to overthrow

VENEZUELA

HEAD OF STATE AND GOVERNMENT
President Hugo Chávez

AREA
352,143 sq mi (slightly more than twice the size of California)

POPULATION
23,542,649

LIFE EXPECTANCY
male: 70.05 years/female: 76.31 years

INFANT MORTALITY RATE
26.17 deaths/1,000 live births

ANNUAL PER CAPITA INCOME
$8,000

LITERACY RATE
91.1%

GDP (GROSS DOMESTIC PRODUCT)
$182.8 billion

GDP GROWTH RATE
-7.2%

INFLATION RATE (CONSUMER PRICES)
20%

INDUSTRIES
Petroleum, iron ore mining, construction materials, food processing, textiles, steel, aluminum, and motor vehicle assembly

Source: *The World Factbook 2000*, published by the Central Intelligence Agency

Pérez—ran for the presidency on a platform of economic reform, an end to government corruption, and the termination of the two-party system. He won with 57 percent of the vote.

The New Venezuela. While Hugo Chávez came to power in a free and fair election, he has since dismantled many of the nation's democratic structures. President Chávez's political ideology, which he calls "Bolivarian Messianism," after the nation's hero, consists of a combination of revolutionary idealism, militarism, and socialism. He designed a new unicameral legislature called the National Constituent Assembly and then manipulated elections for its seats to make sure the representatives would be his supporters. The National Constituent Assembly wrote a new constitution that broadens the responsibilities of the executive branch, making it possible for Chávez to dissolve congress and stay in power until 2013. The constitution also allows for some censorship of the press, thus restricting the media's ability to criticize Chávez's actions. Venezuela's former legislature, its congress, was dissolved, and the Venezuelan people approved the new constitution by referendum in December 1999.

The Rebirth of Military Control. In addition to changing the federal government, Chávez has used the nation's military to

Native Ecuadorans have protested for full recognition of their rights for the past thirty years. Many democracies struggle to sustain full equality for minority groups.

strengthen his power. He has promoted military officials without legislative approval, given regional army commands oversight of locally elected officials, and used armed forces to create jobs in public works. In December 1999, when torrential rains flooded much of the country, President Chávez dispatched troops to troubled areas to rescue survivors and protect property and roads. While he believed his actions were in the spirit of community, some regional governors saw the heavy military presence as evidence of a deteriorating democracy. These fears seemed confirmed in July 2000, when elections for the regional governments were held. After opposition party candidates accused Chávez's party of altering the outcome of the elections, Chávez threatened to use troops to overcome protests and remove elected opposition leaders from office. International observers are also alarmed by the way Chávez has praised communist Cuban dictator Fidel Castro.

Threats to the Rule of Law. Chávez has also depleted the powers of the courts and undermined the rule of law. With the president's approval, the new assembly has given itself the power to dismiss judges and reform the judicial system. The rule of law in Venezuela is also threatened by the South American crime wave. Every month hundreds of people, most of whom are connected to the drug trade, are killed in Venezuela's largest cities. The police and military security forces routinely and arbitrarily detain and torture criminal suspects, and sometimes kill them. Decisions made by the military courts cannot be appealed in the state judicial system, further concentrating military power. Freedom House reports that Venezuela's prisons, among the most violent in the world, hold about 23,000 inmates. Yet less than one third of them have actually been convicted of a crime.

Venezuela Looks Ahead. The United States has an interest in helping Venezuela develop a stable democratic government in order to slow the drug trade and strengthen the economic relationship between the two countries. In recent years, Venezuela has been the leading oil supplier to the United States, and Venezuela hopes to see its oil exports revitalize its stumbling economy. In the first year after Chávez took office, the nation's economy shrunk by 7 percent. Unemployment and inflation have been high. Increased oil exports would thus help boost the nation's economy out of deep recession. In 2000, Ali Rodríguez Araque, Venezuela's energy minister, was appointed president of the Organization of Petroleum Exporting Countries (OPEC). Rodríguez's appointment may positively influence Venezuela's economy by bolstering its standing with the wealthier nations of the world, including the United States.

As in many other emerging democracies, citizens' civil liberties are still challenged in Venezuela. The media are predominantly privately owned, but journalists are supervised by a government broadcasting association and are sometimes intimidated by government officials who want publicity. Labor unions exercise their right to associate freely, but many are closely tied to government leaders and are therefore vulnerable to corruption.

Some progress has been made to acknowledge the rights of groups previously ignored or considered unequal to other citizens. Native Indian populations, who hold few land titles and are often victims of abuse and killings, have received some recognition in the new constitution. They were granted additional legal rights, allowing them to use their language, practice their religion, and organize for social and economic purposes. The Indians hope these new rights will remain protected even as the government moves away from democratic norms.

Despite Venezuela's progress toward establishing democracy in the last few years, a slide back toward autocratic rule jeopardizes its citizens' freedoms. Experts will be carefully watching Venezuela in the future to see whether the nation's citizens continue to support the dismantling of their democratic government or push to regain their political sovereignty.

UGANDA

Ethnic tensions and the pursuit of power fueled generations of conflict in Africa. The continent still suffers from years of colonial domination by the French, Belgians, Portuguese, and British. In establishing their control, these European powers created international boundaries that failed to account for differences in ethnicity and language among the African people. The colonizers also confiscated precious timber, minerals, oil, and other valuable resources for themselves.

Beginning in the 1960s, many African nations gained independence from the colonial powers. In the years since they won their freedom, however, old tribal tensions have reemerged. The new national governments have not consistently been able to meet the needs of the various peoples within each country's borders. Today, Africa is plagued by civil unrest, and the transition to democratic government is, for most nations, an exercise in mediation, patience, and perseverance.

Africa's Bright Spot? Some have called Uganda Africa's bright spot. In his 1908 book, *My African Journey*, Winston Churchill described it as, "the Pearl of Africa." Located in East Africa, and surrounded by nations engaged in bitter ethnic and racial conflicts, Uganda has become a model of stability in a region that many diplomats and development experts expect to be troubled for years to come.

Uganda is one of the smaller African nations, home to only 3 percent of the total African population, in an area approximately the size of Oregon. Despite its abundant natural resources, it is a poor nation. The annual per capita income is about $1,000. Consequently, health care and nutrition are lacking because the people do not have the financial resources to deal effectively with the problems of disease and hunger. In Uganda and throughout Africa, the most fearsome health problem is the prolific spread of AIDS. Despite the success of some recent programs, experts estimate that in some African nations one half of all teenagers will die from AIDS. At present, about one in ten of Uganda's citizens are HIV positive. As Africa's population is lost to this terrible disease, it becomes increasingly difficult for democratic ideals to gain a solid foothold.

A Brutal History. Uganda won independence from Britain in 1962 and, in succeeding years, experienced considerable political instability, largely because of tensions between northern and southern Ugandan ethnic groups. In 1971, the authoritarian president, Milton Obote, was overthrown in a military coup led by armed forces commander Idi Amin. Amin declared himself president, dissolved the parliament, and amended the constitution to grant himself absolute power.

From 1971 to 1978, Amin waged a campaign of terror, killing hundreds of thousands of people, particularly members of the Acholi and Lango tribes from northern Uganda, to which Obote and many of his supporters belonged.

Amin's terrible reign came to an end when he invaded Tanzania in 1978. Amin's army was defeated by Tanzanian forces and Ugandan exiles, who then conducted fraudulent elections in 1980 to return Obote to power. President once again, over the next five years Obote and his supporters from northern Uganda violently attacked critics, who were mostly from ethnic groups in southern Uganda. Obote's security forces attained one of the world's worst human rights records while trying to end an insurgency led by Yoweri Museveni's National Resistance Army (NRA).

A New Government. Obote was ousted by another military coup in 1985, and conditions continued to deteriorate until Yoweri Museveni and his army seized the nation's capital of Kampala in 1986 and assumed control. Museveni's forces installed a government and made him president. Critics of Museveni were concerned that he might become yet another African military dictator. Yet since coming to power, Museveni has made positive changes. The government, which is dominated by his party, the National Resistance Movement (NRM), has ended the human rights abuses of earlier administrations. A 276-seat, unicameral parliament has been established, and a system of local government with locally elected officials has been put into place. Museveni has overseen an expansion in freedoms of the press, reestablished the rule of law, and allowed nongovernmental organizations focusing on human rights issues to operate with relative ease. He is also trying to resolve the nation's ethnic tensions.

In his attempts to restore a sense of national identity and political tranquillity to Uganda, Museveni has used some unique measures. Since 1986, for example, the nation's political system has officially operated without political parties under a plan called the Movement.

Political parties do exist in Uganda, but they are heavily restricted. The constitution states that candidates running for office may not run under political party banners. Further, political parties may not recruit members, hold rallies or delegate conferences, or conduct any other activities that could interfere with the Movement system. President Museveni argues that political parties in Africa form along ethnic or religious lines and therefore undermine the formation of a democratic government. He fears that a multiparty system would only lead to more ethnic conflicts, similar to those waged when Obote and Amin were in power. Critics say Museveni's "no-party democracy" more closely resembles a traditional dictatorship than a modern democracy. Others, however, argue that Museveni's plan has brought the country stability, which has in turn strengthened the economy and elevated the standard of living.

In June 2000, the Movement system was put to a vote in a national referendum. The results were mixed. While 90 percent of voters advocated keeping the system, only half of the country's registered voters cast ballots. Both the Movement supporters and the restricted political parties that had encouraged voters to boycott the referendum, claimed victory. The restricted political parties believed that low-voter turnout signaled the people's desire to move toward an official multiparty system.

Democratic Setbacks. Political power in Uganda has stayed firmly with Museveni's party, the NRM. Important policy decisions are made by Museveni or the legislature without significant public or parliamentary debate, and the NRM has exclusive access to state funds. These advantages have made it easier for the NRM to maintain its hold on the national legislature in elections. Museveni's power is also extensive in the judicial branch. Members of the judiciary are appointed by a judicial commission

UGANDA

HEAD OF STATE AND GOVERNMENT
President Yoweri Museveni

AREA
91,135 sq mi (slightly smaller than Oregon)

POPULATION
23,317,560

LIFE EXPECTANCY
male: 42.22 years/female: 43.67 years

INFANT MORTALITY RATE
93.25 deaths/1,000 live births

ANNUAL PER CAPITA INCOME
$1,060

LITERACY RATE
61.8%

GDP (GROSS DOMESTIC PRODUCT)
$24.2 billion

GDP GROWTH RATE
5.5%

INFLATION RATE (CONSUMER PRICES)
7%

INDUSTRIES
Sugar, brewing, tobacco, cotton textiles, and cement

Source: *The World Factbook 2000*, published by the Central Intelligence Agency

In 1976, Muhammad Yunus, an economics professor in Bangladesh, wanted to find a way to help poor workers become entrepreneurs and move themselves out of poverty. Typically, banks did not give start-up loans to poor workers because they feared that the workers would never be able to repay the loans. Yunus decided to try an experiment. Out of his own pocket, he lent about $26 to a group of forty-two workers. The workers used the money to buy materials for one day's labor making pots and weaving chairs. By the end of their first day, the workers had sold their goods, and shortly thereafter, they repaid Yunus's loan.

Muhammad Yunus used this experience to found Grameen Bank, a new kind of financial institution offering small entrepreneurial loans specifically to those living in poverty. Grameen Bank began a worldwide movement—now known as microcredit. Microcredit, also called microenterprise, helps low-income people start their own businesses.

Over the last decade, many institutions—including banks, nongovernmental organizations, and governments of developed nations—have started to fund microcredit programs in emerging democracies around the world. This innovative approach to ending poverty is helping democracy take root. In nations whose economies were formerly state controlled, microcredit has created new employment opportunities, raised the standard of living, and stimulated economic growth, thus helping stabilize the nations' civic structures from the ground up. Microcredit has been particularly helpful to women, who often go into business in groups, selling goods they have made in their homes. A program run by Zambuko Trust in Zimbabwe enabled its participants, 80 percent of whom are women, to increase their incomes by 25 percent in one year. After two years, the participants' incomes had doubled.

Liba Taylor/Corbis

Women in the West African nation of Ghana sell their goods at market.

named by the president, and the president has influence on the judiciary's rulings.

International organizations that contribute money to Uganda are alarmed by the NRM's control. In 1999, the International Monetary Fund delayed sending an $18 million loan to Uganda, because it feared the money would be misspent.

Respect and Progress. Despite Uganda's no-party system, it has won favor with Western nations for its entry into the world market. The United States considers President Museveni to be one of Africa's brightest and most progressive leaders. Museveni has embraced the principles of capitalism, selling state-owned enterprises to private individuals and groups, seeking foreign investment, and reducing trade tariffs. These initiatives increase the probability of doing business with Western democracies, including the United States. He has also strongly supported the largest foreign investment project in East Africa, a hydroelectric dam on the Nile River. The privatization process has given a tremendous boost to Uganda's economy by increasing the output of goods and services, raising tax revenue, and creating new investment and job opportunities. As evidence of Museveni's positive influence, many cite the fact that Uganda's gross domestic product (GDP) has averaged a growth rate of 7 percent over the last twelve years.

Despite this growth, however, Uganda is less wealthy today than it was thirty years ago, and approximately 40 percent of the nation's population lives in poverty. Corrupt practices take money away from federal projects, and the government has lost international financial aid because of its military spending for both internal and external conflicts.

Ethnic conflict within Uganda's borders has been restricted to the northeast region in recent years, but refugees fleeing the troubles have settled elsewhere in the nation, causing some friction with other groups. Outside of its borders, Uganda has been heavily involved in the ethnic wars of neighboring nations for a variety of reasons. Ugandan forces have assisted rebel groups challenging the government of the Republic of Congo and have played a role in conflicts in Sudan.

Although concerned about the ongoing ethnic conflicts, Western diplomats are counting on President Museveni to serve as a role model to other African leaders and to forge the way to peace and stability in Africa. And while Ugandans disagree over whether to form a multiparty system, many hope their nation's representative democracy will become more free and fair in the future.

THAILAND

East Asia appears to be teeming with democratic potential. Many of the region's nations have expressed interest in developing capitalist economies and representative governments. Experts say South Korea, the Philippines, Taiwan, Malaysia, Nepal, and Thailand are all making substantial progress in becoming democratic nations.

Until 1932, Thailand (known as Siam until 1939) was a pure monarchy. According to tradition, Thais date the founding of their nation to 1238, when

Thai chieftains overthrew their Khmer overlords and established a Thai kingdom. For the next 700 years, Thailand was ruled by a few different royal families. In the nineteenth century, Thai kings were concerned with the European colonization of neighboring Burma and made efforts to negotiate with Western powers in the hope of preserving their nation's independence. The Thai people believe that the diplomatic strengths of their kings, combined with their willingness to modernize and reform the government, made Thailand the only Asian nation able to elude European colonization.

Since the end of World War II, Thailand has enjoyed a close relationship with the United States. When communist revolutions threatened freedom in Burma, Laos, Vietnam, and Cambodia, Thailand actively sought to contain communism's expansion in the region. The United States was grateful for Thailand's cooperation, and today American diplomats recognize its economic and political influence in Asia. In its transition to democracy, Thailand has continued to promote peace, stability, and financial growth in the region by joining the Association of South East Asian Nations (ASEAN). ASEAN promotes business development in Asia, and Thailand plays a key role as a regional financial center.

Kings and Coups. In 1932, a bloodless coup curbed the Thai king's powers and led to the creation of a parliament elected by the people. Although a new democratic system was in place, stability was beyond reach for some time. The nation endured another seventeen coups over the course of the twentieth century, and a series of military governments interspersed with democratic regimes ruled the nation. The coups ended in a flurry of political upheaval at the beginning of the 1990s. In 1991, the army overthrew a corrupt elected government, and parliament appointed the coup leader, General Suchinda Krapayoon, prime minister. In May 1992, massive demonstrations in Bangkok by middle-class citizens, during which soldiers killed more than fifty people, forced Suchinda to resign. In response to the people's demands, Thailand returned to civilian rule.

Today, political power in Thailand lies with the parliament and the prime minister (who is now elected from among parliament's members). However, the military still retains some political influence. Many years of military rule taught the current officers to expect their powers to extend beyond the military's bounds. Thus, democracy in Thailand continues to be undermined by subtle military intervention in government activities. The royal family is also an issue. King Bhumibol Adulyadej, who is well respected by the Thai people, is the head of state and still informally intervenes in the nation's politics.

Trial and Error. As in other new democracies, Thailand's first few elections were neither entirely free nor fair. The 1996 parliamentary elections were marred by fraud and other irregularities. A coalition led by a former army commander, Chavalit Yongchaiyudh, used force to control the election's outcome. Police and soldiers were hired to intimidate voters, candidates bought votes, and violent partisan attacks killed seven people.

When Chavalit was elected prime minister, the nation's economy was weak. Thailand's economy had expanded rapidly between 1985 and 1995, but its strength was diminishing in 1996 because of a decrease in exports, tens of billions of dollars of foreign debt, and a poorly supervised banking system. In 1997, Thailand plunged headfirst into a financial crisis, followed by most of Asia. The financial crisis made unemployment and social problems worse. The trafficking of women throughout Asia for prostitution increased, as did the spread of AIDS.

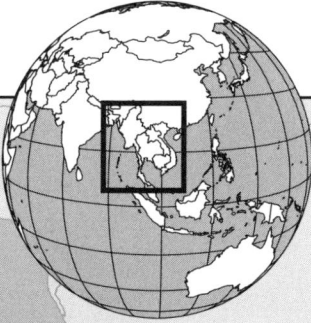

THAILAND

HEAD OF STATE
King Bhumibol Adulyadej

HEAD OF GOVERNMENT
Prime Minister Chuan Leekpai held office through January 2001, when Thaksin Shinawatra, of the Thai Rak Thai Party, was elected with a majority of the vote.

AREA
198,455 sq mi (slightly more than twice the size of Wyoming)

POPULATION
61,230,874

LIFE EXPECTANCY
male: 65.29 years/female: 71.97 years

INFANT MORTALITY RATE
31.48 deaths/1,000 live births

ANNUAL PER CAPITA INCOME
$6,400

LITERACY RATE
93.8%

GDP (GROSS DOMESTIC PRODUCT)
$388.7 billion

GDP GROWTH RATE
4%

INFLATION RATE (CONSUMER PRICES)
2.4%

INDUSTRIES
Tourism, textiles and garments, agricultural processing, beverages, tobacco, cement, and electric appliances

Source: *The World Factbook 2000*, published by the Central Intelligence Agency

Middle-class Thais blamed the financial crisis and social problems on government corruption. They once again used the power of mass demonstrations to demand change. In 1997, the nation's sixteenth constitution since 1932 was drafted with public consultation. It included anticorruption provisions and detailed plans for a new electoral system. In addition, the parliament became a bicameral legislature, currently composed of a 500-seat house of representatives and a 200-seat senate. The new parliament chose Chuan Leekpai to be the nation's prime minister.

A Recovering Economy. Thailand's economy began moving out of the devastating financial crisis near the end of the 1990s. Compared to neighboring nations, the country is peaceful, and it therefore attracts many foreign investors, mostly from Japan, Hong Kong, Taiwan, Singapore, and the United States. Before World War II, Thailand's economy was sustained by rice and rice products. Today, however, the economy is more broad based and less reliant upon agriculture; the manufacturing of goods for export, particularly electronics, is a leading source of national income.

Thailand's recovering economy will be a source of strength for the nation in its movement toward democracy. However, many problems remain. Over the last three decades, the economic boom produced severe disparities in income between the wealthy and the poor. Industrial development was focused in the capital of Bangkok, where only 15 percent of the nation's citizens live. Poor, rural communities are now in need of support, but the nation's infrastructure of roads and communications systems in these areas are too weak to attract business from the cities.

The government so far has been slow to respond to these problems, and some Thais fear that the military is playing too large a role in addressing them. Soldiers in rural areas portray an image of caring for the needy, but they do so to gain leverage in the legislative process. While few believe the military would conduct another coup to regain power, many democracy supporters would like to see constitutional reform to restrict the military's involvement in legislative affairs.

The Rule of Law and Civil Liberties. Like courts in some other emerging democracies, the courts in Thailand are highly corrupt. Wealthy Thai citizens use their influence in court cases. Therefore, not all citizens are treated equally before the law. Democracy advocates are also concerned about the fact that criminal suspects are not guaranteed an attorney for trial. Unlike courts in Venezuela and Uganda, however, Thailand's courts are somewhat more independent of the legislative and administrative branches of government. Some progress has been made for minority groups as well. The Thai Muslim minority has its own Sharia (Islamic court) for civil cases.

The larger concern with regard to the rule of law in Thailand is its corrupt and poorly trained police force. The police force is battling an ever-increasing and violent drug trade covering much of the region. To deal with the crisis, the police have been known to execute drug traffickers and other criminal suspects. The treatment of women is also disturbing, both in immigration centers and prisons, where female detainees say rape by police is common.

With regard to civil liberties, Thailand has implemented some measures to limit freedoms of expression. The constitution and several laws specifically prohibit speech that incites disturbances or that is in favor of a communist government. All five national television stations and most radio stations are owned by the government or the military. Journalists are not free to criticize the government and its policies; the press censors itself when reporting on sensitive topics such as the military, the monarchy, and the judiciary.

Thailand's transition to democracy is not ensured, as the monarch continues to play a small political role, and the military looms like a dim shadow over the government's affairs. Nevertheless, Western nations are inspired by initiatives the middle class has taken to express its desire for further democratic change. Energetic marching in the streets has been an effective instrument of democratic change in Thailand. In the coming years, Thais hope the growing economy will further stabilize the democratic forms already in place and empower the nation to find more progressive solutions to the social problems that remain.

COMMON BONDS

As the world settles into the twenty-first century, citizens of emerging democracies are looking to improve and stabilize their democratic governments. The nations of Russia, Venezuela, Uganda, and Thailand illustrate that while a democratic government may technically be in place, growing and maintaining a democratic nation is an ongoing challenge.

The experiences of Venezuela, Uganda, and Thailand, for instance, have shown how an uncontrolled military can stifle a new democracy's growth. When the military is not subject to civilian control, citizens' safety is jeopardized and military coups may result.

Russia is currently struggling to motivate citizens to participate in the political process. For the new Russian democracy to succeed, citizens will need to accept democratic principles and understand their potential to generate political change. Admittedly, encouraging citizens to seek democratic change when the economy is poor is difficult, but in time, free-market economies can work in harmony with democratic systems. Democracy promoters hope Russian citizens will keep faith in their new democratic and capitalistic systems and encourage their growth.

All of these democracies struggle with the negative effects of crime, corruption, and restrictions on citizens' civil liberties. Experts say these nations must develop stronger civil societies and judicial systems, end human rights abuses, and seek greater cooperation with the more-established democracies of the world. In the years to come, democracy experts also hope advancements in technology will make the transition to democracy easier. Above all, the exchange of democratic ideas is critical to the growth of democracy in these nations.

POSSIBILITIES

Thanks to increased technology and state-of-the-art communications systems, democratic ideas are now filtering into countries that previously seemed entirely closed-off. These nations are called pre-transition nations—they show democratic potential. China and Iran are two such nations.

China. For more than fifty years, China has been a communist nation, and its citizens have lacked any democratic means to change their government. The Chinese Communist Party holds all power and severely restricts citizens' freedoms of religion, association, speech, and press. This totalitarian government also uses the judiciary as a tool of state control, imprisoning people who disagree with government policies.

For these reasons, many have thought that reform in China was nearly impossible. However, changes in the Chinese economy over the last few years have led to increased internal pressure for popular sovereignty. In the mid-1990s, as the Chinese economy rapidly deteriorated, foreign investment dwindled, domestic consumption decreased, and exports slowed. Income inequalities widened, and rural areas became even more isolated from the advances of the modern age.

In response to these conditions, Chinese citizens have staged protests. While the press is tightly controlled by the government, the media has begun, in subtle ways, to discuss the issues plaguing the nation. Without directly mentioning the ruling Communist Party, non-political talk shows and tabloid magazines report on inefficient government agencies, environmental damage, and official corruption. Outside observers say that as China's press becomes more vocal, and as citizens, via the Internet for example, seek information regarding popular rule in the rest of the world, democratic ideals will become more visible to

Journalists marching in China's Tiananmen Square in May 1989 borrow a famous phrase to convey their support for prodemocracy reforms. The brutal crackdown on these protesters led to a decrease in activism in subsequent years; however, public interest in democratic freedom has remained strong.

Reuters/Carl Ho/Archive Photos

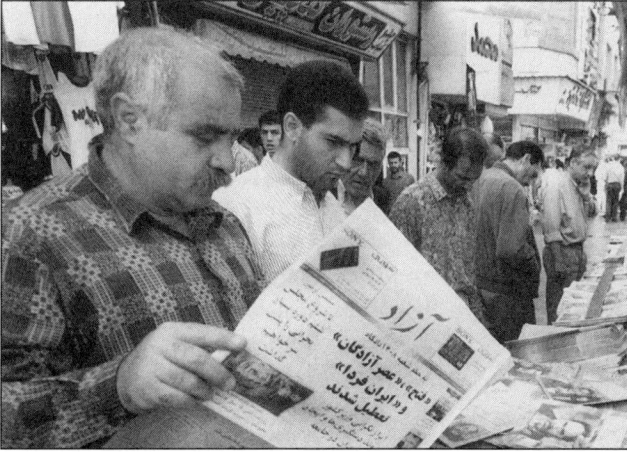

In 2000, Iranian reformers and hardliners battled over freedom of the press. The judiciary banned or suspended publication of many prodemocracy newspapers such as *Azad (Free)*. Here, a man reads the last edition printed before the crackdown.

and the president and states that all laws must be in accordance with the teaching of Islam. The nation's supreme religious leader, Ayatolah Ali Khamenei, gives the final word in all state affairs.

In 1997, as Iran's abundant oil reserves declined, inflation and unemployment soared. This led to a decrease in per capita income and disgruntled citizens pushed for change.

Chinese citizens and the idea of democracy will become more appealing. Observers predict that once citizens accept democratic principles and acknowledge their own potential for change, internal pressure for democracy will topple the communist regime.

Iran. Like China, Iran also faces pressures from internal reformists who are pushing for more liberty under the nation's stringent Islamic system. Iran is a theocracy—a nation whose government is controlled by religious clergy claiming to have divine authority to rule. Iran became a theocracy in 1979, when the hereditary monarch, Shah Mohammad Reza Pahlavi, fled Iran among growing political and religious unrest. The Ayatollah Ruhollah Khomeini then returned from exile to form the world's first Islamic republic. Iran wrote a constitution that provides for direct elections of the parliament

Mohammad Khatami, a former culture minister who had been forced out of the government in 1992 for being too liberal, ran for the presidency on a platform of economic reform, rule of law, civil society, and improved foreign relations. He was elected in a landslide.

While he is still bound by the authority of the religious leader Khamenei, President Khatami has been able to push for moderate reforms. Some prodemocracy dissidents requesting more civil liberties have been allowed to speak out, and Iran is now attracting foreign investment and mending its relations with the West. Britain has agreed to exchange ambassadors with Iran, while the United States has dropped food and medicine from its sanctions against Iran and lowered its standing on the list of state sponsors of terrorism. At a United Nations gathering in September 2000, President Khatami said, "Democratic principles have gradually become the criteria of good governance domestically. They deserve to become the new norm governing global interactions."

DEMOCRACY'S NEXT ROUND

Today, many nations of the world have embraced democracy and its principles of freedom, justice, and the rule of law. Yet each new democracy has also learned that implementing democratic ideals can be long and tiring. Building a democracy is like constructing a home. If it is built well, it will endure. If not, it will fall. While a democracy is being constructed, careful attention must be paid to ensure that each part fits together smoothly. For a new democracy, building the foundation and infrastructure of a government that truly represents the will of the people is an enormous challenge.

First, a new democracy must adopt and respect the democratic requirements of popular sovereignty: free and fair elections; the rule of law; governmental autonomy; inclusive citizenship; universal suffrage; and the freedoms of expression, association, and information. Then, its citizens must decide how to form the government. Will it have a written constitution? How will the members of its assembly, administration, and courts be chosen? Who will be the head of state? And finally, how will citizens sustain the new democratic government once it is in place? Democracy experts ask these questions every day to evaluate the progress of nations in transition. A new democracy must focus its efforts on building accountable state institutions and a strong civil society to make sure the government truly represents the desires of the nation's people.

The optimism of the late 1980s and the early 1990s has been dimmed by the realization that many countries trying to establish democratic governments are plagued by issues that continue to stifle growth. Poor economies, corruption, social instability, and military control are just a few of the challenges facing new democracies. Despite these obstacles, however, democracy continues to spread to the far corners of the globe. And as the people of even more nations carve out new ways of implementing the democratic process, the story of democracy will continue to unfold.

FOR FURTHER READING

The following books and articles will provide further information on some of the topics covered in *Building a Democratic Nation: Governments in Transition.*

Bunbongkarn, Suchit. "Thailand's Successful Reforms." *Journal of Democracy* 10, no. 4 (1999): 54–68.

Carothers, Thomas. *Aiding Democracy Abroad: The Learning Curve.* Washington, D.C.: Carnegie Endowment for International Peace, 1999.

"China Today." *Congressional Quarterly Researcher* 10, no. 27. (August 4, 2000): entire issue.

Close Up Foundation. *International Relations: Understanding the Behavior of Nations.* 4th ed. Alexandria, Virginia: Close Up Foundation, 2001.

Crawley, Mike. "Economic Policy Keeps Museveni in West's Favor." *The Christian Science Monitor,* August 2, 2000: 7.

Dahl, Robert A. *On Democracy.* New Haven, Connecticut: Yale University Press, 1998.

Fedorov, Yuri. "Democratization and Globalization: The Case of Russia." *Working Papers—Democracy and Rule of Law Project, Global Policy Program.* no. 13 (May 2000). Washington, D.C.: Carnegie Endowment for International Peace. www.ceip.org/files/Publications/demandglob.asp?p=1&from=pubdate

Goldman, Minton F., comp. *Global Studies: Russia, The Eurasian Republics, and Central/Eastern Europe.* 8th ed. Guilford, Connecticut: Dushkin/McGraw-Hill, 2000.

Goodwin, Paul B., Jr., comp. *Global Studies: Latin America.* 9th ed. Guilford, Connecticut: Dushkin/McGraw-Hill, 2000.

Karatnycky, Adrian, ed. *Freedom in the World—The Annual Survey of Political Rights and Civil Liberties 1999–2000.* New York, New York: Freedom House, 2000.

MacLeod, Scott and Azadeh Moaveni. "Iran's New Revolution." *TIME* 155, no. 24 (June 12, 2000): 37–42.

Norton, James K. *Global Studies: India and South Asia.* 4th ed. Guilford, Connecticut: Dushkin/McGraw-Hill, 1999.

Ramsay, F. Jeffress, comp. *Global Studies: Africa.* 8th ed. Guilford, Connecticut: Dushkin/McGraw-Hill, 1999.

Rohter, Larry. "A Combative Leader Shapes Venezuela to a Leftist Vision." *New York Times,* July 28, 1999: A1/A6.

Smith, Dan. *The State of the World Atlas.* 6th ed. New York, New York: Penguin Putnam Inc., 1999.

ALSO AVAILABLE FROM CLOSE UP PUBLISHING

International Relations:
Understanding the Behavior of Nations

U.S. Response: The Making of U.S. Foreign Policy (simulation)

The Breakup of the Soviet Union:
U.S.-Russian Relations Ten Years Later

Current Issues: Critical Policy Choices
Facing the Nation and the World

Ordinary Americans: Vietnam (video)

Ordinary Americans: The Red Scare (video)

Ordinary Americans: The Civil Rights Movement (video)

Ordinary Americans:
U.S. History Through the Eyes of Everyday People

The Bill of Rights: A User's Guide

The First Amendment: America's Blueprint for Tolerance